MW01232980

KALI LINUX

Kali Linux for beginners learn about Penetration Testing Operating System + Ethical Hacking.

1 BOOK OF 5

5

Introduction

Kali Linux is the world's most effective and famous penetration testing platform, used by safety specialists in an extensive range of specializations, which include penetration testing out, forensics, reverse engineering, and vulnerability assessment. It is the fruit of years of refinement and the end result of a continuous evolution of the platform, from Whoppix to WHAX, to go into reverse, and now to an entire penetration testing framework leveraging many capabilities of Debian GNU/Linux and the vibrant open supply network global. Kali Linux has no longer been constructed to be a simple collection of gear, but alternatively a flexible framework that expert penetration testers, security fanatics, college students, and amateurs can personalize to fit their precise needs. Kali Linux is not merely a set of numerous statistics protection tools which might be established on a trendy Debian base and preconfigured to get you up and walking proper away. To get the maximum out of Kali, it is critical to have a radical knowledge of its powerful Debian GNU/Linux underpinnings and getting to know how you could position them to use on your surroundings. Although Kali is decidedly multiple reasons, it is in most cases designed to useful resource in penetration testing out. The goal of this book is not always simplest that will help you experience at home when you use Kali Linux, but also to assist enhance your expertise and streamline your revel in in order that whilst you are engaged in a penetration check and time is of the essence, you won't want to fear about dropping valuable minutes to install new software or permit a new network provider. On this book, we are able to introduce you first to Linux, then we are able to dive deeper as we introduce you to the nuances unique to Kali Linux, so you recognize precisely what goes on beneath the hood. That is priceless knowhow to have, in particular whilst you are attempting to work below tight time constraints. It isn't always uncommon to require this intensity of expertise while you are getting set up, troubleshooting a trouble, struggling to bend a system in your will, parsing output from a tool, or leveraging Kali in a larger scale surroundings.

The Kali Linux project started out quietly in 2012, whilst Offensive protection determined that they wanted to update their venerable back off Linux undertaking, which turned into manually maintained, with something that would end up a true Debian derivative, complete with all the required infrastructure and improved packaging techniques. The choice changed into made to construct Kali on pinnacle of the Debian distribution due to the fact it is far widely recognized for its quality, balance, and huge selection of to be had software. The primary release (model 1.0) came about twelve months later, in March 2013, and become primarily based on Debian 7 "Wheezy", Debian's solid distribution at the time. In that first 12 months of development, they packaged hundreds of penetration testing related applications and constructed the infrastructure. Even though the number of packages is vast, the application listing has been meticulously curated, dropping programs that not worked or that duplicated functions already to be had in better programs.

Throughout the 2 years following model 1.0, Kali launched many incremental updates, increasing the variety of to be had packages and enhancing hardware aid, thanks to more recent kernel related. With some investment in continuous integration, it was ensured that everyone important programs had been kept in an installable nation and that customized live pictures (an indicator of the distribution) could usually be created. In 2015, while Debian 8 "Jessie" came out, the work to rebase Kali Linux on top. While Kali Linux 1.x averted the GNOME Shell (counting on GNOME Fallback as an alternative), on this version it was decided to include and decorate it: the few GNOME Shell extensions to collect lacking capabilities, maximum appreciably the packages menu. The result of that work became Kali Linux 2.0, posted in August 2015. In parallel, it elevated the efforts to make certain that Kali Linux always has the new version of all penetration testing out packages. Unfortunately, that aim changed into a chunk at odds with the usage of Debian Stable as a base for the distribution, as it required us to backport many packages. That is because of the reality that Debian solid puts a priority on the steadiness of the software program, often causing an extended put off from the discharge of an upstream

7

update to while it is far included into the distribution. Given our investment in continuous integration, it became quite a natural pass to rebase Kali Linux on top of Debian Testing so that it was ought to benefit from the cutting-edge version of all Debian packages as quickly as they have been to be had. Debian testing has a miles more aggressive update cycle, which is greater compatible with the philosophy of Kali Linux. This is, in essence, the idea of Kali Rolling. Whilst the rolling distribution has been to be had for quite some time, Kali 2016.1 changed into the primary launch to officially embrace the rolling nature of that distribution: when you set up the day Kali release, your system without a doubt tracks the Kali Rolling distribution and every unmarried day you get new updates. Inside the past, Kali releases were snapshots of the underlying Debian distribution with Kaliprecise packages injected into it. A rolling distribution has many advantages, but it additionally comes with multiple demanding situations, both for those folks who are constructing the distribution and for the users who have to cope with a continuous float of updates and every so often backwards incompatible modifications. This book pursuits to present you the understanding required to deal with everything you could come upon while coping with your Kali Linux set up.

Chapter 1

1.1 Kali Relationship with Debian

The Kali Linux distribution is primarily based on Debian Testing. Consequently, most of the packages to be had in Kali Linux come directly from this Debian repository. At the same time as Kali Linux relies heavily on Debian, it's also absolutely independent within the experience that we've got our personal infrastructure and preserve the liberty to make any adjustments we need.

1.1.1 Package Flow

At the Debian side, the individuals are operating each day on updating applications and importing them to the Debian risky distribution (unstable is also called sid). From there, programs migrate to the Debian testing out distribution once the most difficult bugs had been taken out. The migration process additionally guarantees that no dependencies are broken in Debian testing out. The purpose is that testing is continually in a usable (or maybe releasable!) State. Debian testing goals align quite properly with the ones of Kali Linux, so we picked it because the base. To add the Kali particular applications within the distribution, we observe a twostep procedure.
First, we take Debian testing out and fore inject our own Kali applications (located in our kali dev repository) to construct the kali dev repository. This repository will break now and again: for instance, our Kali unique packages may not be installable until they had been recompiled against more recent libraries. In different situations, applications that we've forked may additionally be up to date, both to come to be installable once more, or to restoration the install ability of another bundle that relies upon on a more modern version of the

forked package deal. Anyhow, kali dev is not for end users. Kali rolling is the distribution that Kali Linux users are predicted to track and is constructed out of kali dev within the identical manner that Debian testing out is built out of Debian volatile. Packages migrate simplest while all dependencies may be glad within the target distribution.

1.1.2. Management of Difference with Debian

As a layout selection, we attempt to minimize the wide variety of forked packages as a lot as feasible. However, in an effort to put into effect some of Kali's unique functions, a few modifications need to be made. To limit the impact of these changes, we strive to ship them upstream, both via integrating the function directly, or through including the desired hooks so that it is straightforward to enable the desired features without further editing the upstream programs themselves.

The Kali package Tracker enables us to keep track of our divergence with Debian. At any time, we will look up which package has been forked and whether it's miles in sync with Debian, or if an update is needed. All our programs are maintained in Git repositories web hosting a Debian branch and a Kali department aspect with the aid of aspect. Thanks to this, updating a forked package deal is an easy step technique: replace the Debian branch after which merge it into the Kali department. While the range of forked packages in Kali is distinctly low, the range of additional packages is as an alternative excessive: in January 2021 there were almost 500. Maximum of these packages are free software complying with the Debian unfastened software program Guidelines and our final aim would be to maintain the ones packages within Debian on every occasion possible. This is why we attempt to comply with the Debian Policy and to follow the coolest packaging practices utilized in Debian. Sadly, there also are pretty a few exceptions in which right packaging turned into nearly not possible to create. Because of time being scarce, few packages had been pushed to Debian.

1.2 Use Cases and Purpose

While Kali's awareness may be fast summarized as "penetration testing and protection auditing", there are numerous special tasks worried behind the ones activities. Kali Linux is built as a platform, as it includes many tools masking very distinct use cases (although they may absolutely be used in mixture for the duration of a penetration take a look at).

As an instance, Kali Linux may be used on various styles of computers: obviously on the desktops of penetration testers, however additionally on servers of system directors wishing to display their net paintings, on the workstations of forensic analysts, and more , on stealthy embedded de vices, generally with ARM cpus, that may be dropped within the range of a wireless community or plugged inside the desktop of target customers. Many ARM systems are also ideal attack systems because of their small form elements and occasional power necessities. Kali Linux also can be deployed in the cloud to fast construct a farm of password cracking systems and on mobile phones and pills to permit for truly transportable penetration trying out. But that is not all; penetration testers also need servers: to use collaboration software inside a campaigns, to run vulnerability scanning equipment, and different associated activities.

As soon as you've got booted Kali, you will fast discover that Kali Linux's important menu is organized by theme across the various styles of obligations and activities which can be applicable for penetration testers and different information protection specialists as shown in Figure.

Figure 1.1

Kali Linux

These tasks and activities consists of:

- **Information Gathering:** Collecting data about the target network and its structure, discovering computer systems, their running systems, and the services that they run. Identifying potentially sensitive elements of the information system. Extracting all styles of listings from jogging directory services.
- **Vulnerability evaluation:** speedy testing out whether a local or remote system is tormented by some of known vulnerabilities or insecure configurations. Vulnerability scanners use databases containing heaps of signatures to discover capacity vulnerabilities.
- **Internet utility analysis:** figuring out misconfigurations and safety weaknesses in internet applications. It's miles important to identify and mitigate these problems for the reason that the general public avail potential of those programs makes them ideal goals for attackers.
- **Database evaluation:** From square injection to attacking credentials, database attacks are a not unusual vector for attackers. Tools that check for attack vectors starting from sq. Injection to data extraction and evaluation can be discovered here.
- **Password attacks:** Authentication structures are usually a pass to assault vector. Many beneficial tools may be located here,

from online password attack equipment to offline attacks in opposition to the encryption or hashing systems.

- **Wireless attacks:** The pervasive nature of WIFI networks way that they may constantly be a generally attacked vector. With its extensive variety of aid for multiple wireless playing cards, Kali is an obvious choice for assaults against more than one sorts of WIFI networks.
- **Reverse Engineering:** reverse engineering is an interest with many functions. In help of offensive activities, it's miles one of the primary methods for vulnerability identification and make the most improvement. On the protecting side, it is used to research malware employed in targeted assaults. On this capacity, the aim is to pick out the competencies of a given piece of tradecraft.
- **Exploitation tool:** Exploiting or taking benefit of a (previously diagnosed) vulnerability, lets in you to advantage manage of a remote system (or tool). This access can then be used for further privilege escalation assaults, both regionally locally at the compromised system, or on different systems on hand on its nearby network. This category includes a number of gear and utilities that simplify the manner of writing your own exploits.
- **Sniffing & Spoofing:** Gaining access to the data as they travel across the network is often advantageous for an attacker. Right here you can discover spoofing tools that will let you impersonate a valid person as well as sniffing tools that will let you seize and examine statistics proper off the twine. Whilst used together, these gear can be very effective.
- **Post Exploitation:** Once you have gained access to a system, you will often want to maintain that degree of get right of entry to or expand manipulate by using laterally transferring across the community. Equipment that help in those dreams are found right here.
- **Forensics:** Forensic Linux live boot environments had been very famous for years now. Kali incorporates a huge range of famous Linux based totally forensic tools permitting you to do

everything from preliminary triage, to information imaging, to complete evaluation and case control.

- **Reporting equipment:** A penetration check is handiest whole once the findings have been stated. This category carries equipment to assist collate the information amassed from data collecting tools, find out nonobvious relationships, and produce the entirety together in diverse reviews.

- **Social Engineering tools:** whilst the technical aspect is properly secured, there may be regularly the possibility of exploiting human conduct as an attack vector. Given the proper impact, people can frequently be caused to take moves that compromise the security of the surroundings. Did the USB key that the secretary just plugged in contain an innocent PDF? Or become it additionally a malicious program that established a backdoor? Turned into the banking internet site the accountant just logged into the predicted website or a great replica used for phishing functions? This category contains tools that resource in these forms of attacks.

Chapter 2

2.1 Kali Linux Main Features

Kali Linux is a Linux distribution that contains its personal collection of loads of software program tool specifically tailor made for their target customers penetration testers and other protection professionals. It also comes with an installation software to completely setup Kali Linux as the main operating system on any pc. That is quite similar to all other existing Linux distributions but there are different features that differentiate Kali Linux, lots of that are tailored to the precise needs of penetration testers.

2.1.1 Live System

Alongside the main installer ISO images, Kali Linux offers a separate live ISO picture to download. This lets you to use Kali Linux as a bootable live system. In different words, you can use Kali Linux without installing it, just by booting the ISO picture (normally after having copied the photo onto a USB key). The live system carries the tool most usually utilized by penetration testers, so even in case your daily system is not Kali Linux, you may definitely insert the disk or USB key and reboot to run Kali. But remember that the default configuration will now not keep adjustments among reboots. If you configure endurance with a USB key, then you may tweak the gadget on your liking (adjust config files, store reports, improve software program, and installation extra programs, as an example), and the changes could be retained across reboots.

2.1.2 Completely Customizable

Kali Linux is constructed by way of penetration testers for penetration testers; however, we take into account that not everyone will trust our design choices or preference of equipment to include by using default. With this in thoughts, we constantly make certain that Kali Linux is easy to personalize based on your personal wishes and likeness. To this end, we publish the live build configuration used to build the legit Kali images so that you can customize it for your liking. It is very clean to start from this published configuration and put in force numerous modifications primarily based in your desires way to the flexibility of live build.

Stay construct consists of many features to regulate the installed system, installation supplementary files, install additional applications, run arbitrary instructions, and trade the values presided to deb conf.

2.1.3 Custom Linux Kernel

Kali Linux continually gives a customized current Linux kernel, based at the model in Debian unstable. This ensures solid hardware aid, in particular for a huge range of WIFI systems. The kernel is patched for WIFI injection assist because many WIFI security evaluation gear depend upon this selection. For the reason that many hardware system require up to date firmware files (observed in /lib/firmware/), Kali installs all of them by default which include the firmware available in Debian's not free section. The ones aren't set up with the aid of default in Debian, because they are closed supply and hence not part of Debian proper.

2.1.4 Usable on a Huge Range of ARM Systems

Kali Linux gives binary applications for the armel, armhf, and arm64 ARM architectures. Way to the effortlessly installable pictures provided by using Offensive security, Kali Linux can be deployed on many exciting systems, from smartphones and drugs to wireless routers and computers of numerous styles and sizes.

2.1.5 A Trustable Operating System

Users of a safety distribution rightfully need to recognize that it could be depended on and that it has been evolved in undeniable sight, allowing all people to look at the supply code. Kali Linux is evolved via a small team of knowledgeable developers running transparently and following the excellent protection practices: they add signed supply packages, which might be then built on devoted construct daemons. The applications are then check summed and disbursed as part of a signed repository. The work done out at the applications can be completely reviewed through the packaging Git repositories (which incorporate signed tags) which might be used to build the Kali source programs. The evolution of every package deal also can be observed thru the Kali package tracker.

2.1.6 Forensic Mode

In general, whilst doing forensic paintings on a system, you need to avoid any hobby that would modify the information on the analyzed gadget in any way. Alas, current computing system environments have a tendency to interfere with this objective by means of trying to automount any disk(s) they detect. To avoid this conduct, Kali Linux has a forensics mode that can be enabled from the boot menu: it's going to disable all such features. The live system is specifically beneficial for forensics functions, due to the fact it is feasible to reboot any desktop into a Kali Linux system without getting access to or enhancing its hard disks.

2.2 Policies

At the same time as Kali Linux strives to follow the Debian policy whenever feasible, there are some areas in which we made significantly exceptional layout choices because of the unique needs of protection professionals.

2.2.1 Network Services Disabled via Default

In contrast to Debian, Kali Linux disables any established provider that could concentrate on a public internet work interface by using default, such as HTTP and SSH. The intent at the back of this selection is to reduce exposure at some stage in a penetration check whilst it's far unfavorable to announce your presence and risk detection due to unexpected network interactions. You can still manually allow any offerings of your selecting by way of going for walks sudo systemctl permit carrier.

2.2.2 Curated series of packages

Debian ambitions to be the normal running gadget and places very few limits on what receives packaged, supplied that each bundle has a maintainer. By way of comparison, Kali Linux does not package every penetration trying out tool available. As an alternative, we purpose to offer most effective the best freely licensed tools masking maximum obligations that a penetration tester may want to perform. Kali builders working as penetration testers force the selection procedure and we leverage their experience and expertise to make enlightened selections. In a few instances this is a depend on reality, but there are other, more difficult alternatives that honestly come right down to private choice.

Right here are some of the factors considered while a new application receives evaluated:

- The adequate usefulness of the application in context of penetration testing
- The distinctive unique functionality of the features of application.
- The license of the application
- The resource application requirements

Retaining an up to date and beneficial penetration checking out system repository is a challenging mission. We welcome system recommendations inside a dedicated class (new tool requests) in the Kali bug Tracker. New tool requests are first class received when the submission is properly offered, which includes an explanation of why the tool is useful, the way it compares to different similar programs, and so on.

Chapter 3

3.1 Fundamentals of Linux

The term "Linux" is often used to refer the entire running system, however in reality, Linux is the operating system kernel, that's commenced by way of the boot loader, that's itself commenced through the BIOS/UEFI. The kernel assumes a position much like that of a conductor in an orchestra it ensures coordination among hardware and software program. This role consists of coping with hardware, processes, customers, permissions, and the report gadget. The kernel gives a commonplace base to all other programs on the system and commonly runs in ring 0, also known as kernel space.
The User Space We use the term user space to lump collectively everything that happens outside of the kernel. Some of the programs running in user space are many core utilities from the GNU project, maximum of which might be meant to be run from the command line.

3.2 Driving hardware

The kernel is tasked, first and primary, with controlling the desktop's hardware additives. It detects and configures them when the pc powers on, or when a system is inserted or removed (as an example, a USB system). It additionally makes them to be had to higher stage software program, via a simplified programming interface, so programs can take benefit of gadgets without having to address information along with which extension slot a choice board is plugged into. The programming interface also presents an abstraction layer; this allows video conferencing software program, for example, to apply a webcam irrespective of its maker and version. The software program can use the Video for Linux (V4L) interface and the kernel will translate function calls of the interface into actual hardware commands wished by way of the unique webcam in use. The kernel exports facts about detected hardware via the /proc/ and /sys/ virtual record systems. Programs frequently get admission to gadgets by way of way of files created within /dev/. Precise files represent disk drives (for instance, /dev/sda), walls (/dev/sda1), mice (/dev/enter/mouse0), keyboards (/dev/input/event0), sound cards (/dev/snd/*), serial ports (/dev/ttys*), and different components.

There are two forms of system files: block and character. The former has traits of a block of information: It has a finite size, and you could get right of entry to bytes at any function inside the block. The latter behaves like a drift of characters. You can study and write characters, but you cannot seek to given role/position and trade arbitrary bytes. To find out the form of a given tool report, check out the first letter inside the output of ls -l. It's far either b, for block systems, or c, for character systems:

```
$       ls      -l      /dev/sda                        /dev/ttys0
brw-rw---- 1 root disk 8,   0   May 24 07:44 /dev/sda
Crw-rw---- 1 root dialout 4, 64 May 30 06:59 /dev/ttys0
```

As you may expect, disk drives and partitions use block systems, while mouse, keyboard, and serial ports use individual gadgets. In each instances, the programming interface consists of system specific commands that can be invoked through the ioctl system name.

3.3 Unifying report systems

File systems are an outstanding factor of the kernel. Unix like systems merge all the record stores into a single hierarchy, which lets in users and packages to access statistics via knowing its place within that hierarchy. The starting point of this hierarchical tree is known as the basis, represented via the "/" person. This listing can contain named subdirectories. As an example, the home subdirectory of / is called /home/. This subdirectory can, in turn, contain other subdirectories, and so forth. Every listing also can contain files, wherein the information could be saved. Thus, /domestic/kali/desktop/hiya.txt refers to a report named hiya.txt stored in the desktop subdirectory of the kali subdirectory of the house directory, gift in the root. The kernel interprets between this naming system and the storage location on a disk. Not like different systems, Linux possesses simplest one such hierarchy, and it may integrate information from several disks. This sort of disks becomes the foundation, and the others are hooked up on directories in the hierarchy (the Linux command is called mount). Those different disks are then available under the mount points. This permits storing users' domestic directories (historically stored within /domestic/) on a separate tough disk, for you to include the kali listing (together with domestic directories of other customers). Once you mount the disk on /domestic/, these directories become available at their regular locations, and paths along with /domestic/kali/desktop/hey.txt keep working.

There are many file system formats, corresponding to many ways of bodily storing records on disks. The most widely known are ext2, ext3, and ext4, but others exist. For example, VFAT is the filesystem that was historically used by DOS and Microsoft windows operating structures. Linux's support for VFAT permits tough disks to be reachable underneath Kali in addition to below Microsoft windows. Anyhow, you need to prepare a file system on a disk before you can mount it and this operation is called formatting. Instructions which includes mkfs.ext4 (in which mkfs stands for make filesystem) handle formatting. These instructions require, as a parameter, a tool record representing the partition to be formatted (as an example, /dev/sda1, the primary partition on the first drive). This operation is damaging and must be run handiest once, unless you want to wipe a filesystem and start clean.

There are also network filesystems which include NFS, which do no longer store statistics on a nearby disk. Instead, facts is transmitted through the community to a server that shops and retrieves them on demand. Thanks to the file system abstraction, you don't ought to fear about how this disk is attached, since the files continue to be available of their normal hierarchical manner.

3.4 Managing Progress

A procedure is a running example of a program, which requires memory to store both the program itself and its working records. The kernel is in fee of making and tracking processes. Whilst an application runs, the kernel first sets apart some reminiscence, hundreds the executable code from the record gadget into it, and then begins the code jogging. It keeps facts approximately this manner, the most visible of that's an identification wide variety called the process identifier (PID). Like most modern working systems, those with Unix like kernels, inclusive of Linux, are capable of multi-tasking. In different phrases, they permit the system to run many techniques at the same time. There's definitely only one going for walks procedure at someone time, however the kernel divides CPU time into small slices and runs each technique in flip. Due to the fact that these time slices are very quick (inside the millisecond range), they invent the advent of procedures walking in parallel, despite the fact that they may be lively handiest in the course of their time c language and are idle the relaxation of the time. The kernel's activity is to regulate its scheduling mechanisms to hold that appearance, while maximizing international system performance. If the time slices are too long, the utility may not appear as responsive as favored. Too quick, and the system loses time with the aid of switching duties too often. These choices may be subtle with processed priorities, wherein high precedence methods will run for longer durations and with greater common time slices than low priority approaches.

Multi-Processor System: The limitation described above, of handiest one process running at a time, doesn't usually apply: the actual limit is that there can be best one walking technique in step with processor middle. Multi-processor, multi core, or hyper threaded systems allow numerous methods to run in parallel. The equal time cutting system is used, although, to deal with cases in which there are more lively processes than to be had processor cores. This isn't always unusual: a simple system, even a typically idle one, nearly continually has tens of running processes.

The kernel permits several impartial times of the equal program to run, however every is authorized to get entry to handiest its very own time slices and memory. Their fact for that reason remains impartial.

3.5 Rights management

Unix like structures support multiple customers and agencies and allow control of permissions. Most of the time, a manner is recognized via the user who started out it. That technique is handiest accepted to take actions accepted for its owner. For example, starting a file requires the kernel to check the method identification towards get entry to permissions.

Chapter 4

4.1 Installation

4.2 Requirements for Installation

The installation requirements for Kali Linux vary depending on what you would like to install. At the low end, you can installation Kali as a simple at ease Shell (SSH) server with no computer, the usage of as little as 128 MB of RAM (512 MB endorsed) and 2 GB of disk space. At the higher quit, in case you choose to installation the default Xfce computing system and the kali Linux default metapackage, you ought to absolutely aim for at least 2048 MB of RAM and 20 GB of disk space. Besides the RAM and tough disk necessities, your pc needs to have a CPU supported via at the least one of the amd64, i386, or arm64 architectures.

4.3 Installation on a Hard Drive

On this segment, we count on which you have a bootable USB drive or DVD and which you booted from it to start the installation procedure.

4.4. Plain Installation

First, we can take a look at a standard Kali set up, with an unencrypted file system.

4.4.1 Booting and starting the Installer

As soon as the BIOS/UEFI has started booting from the USB force or DVD ROM, the iso Linux boot loader menu seems, as shown in determine 4.1, "Boot display screen" . At this stage, the Linux kernel is not but loaded; this menu lets in you to choose the kernel to boot and input optional parameters to be transferred to it inside the procedure. The usage of the arrow keys to do a fashionable installation, both pick out Graphical installation or deploy (for traditional textual content mode), then press the enter key to provoke the remainder of the setup procedure. Each menu entry hides a selected boot command line, which can be configured as wanted with the aid of pressing the Tab key before validating the access and booting.

Figure 4.1

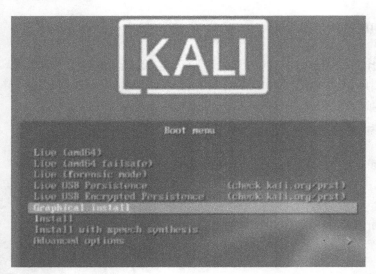

Once booted, the setup program courses you step by step through the procedure. We can take a look at every of those steps in detail. We are able to cowl set up from a popular Kali Linux stay photo, installations from a mini. Iso may additionally appearance barely one of a kind. We are able to additionally cope with graphical mode set up, however the only difference from traditional textual content mode installation is the arrival. The variations pose equal questions and gift equal alternatives.

4.4.2 Selecting the Language

As shown in figure 4.2, "selecting the Language", the installation program starts in English, but the first step allows you to pick the language with a view to be used for the relaxation of the installation process. This language desire is also used to outline extra relevant default selections in subsequent levels (considerably the keyboard layout).

Navigating with the keyboard a few steps inside the setup procedure require you to go into statistics. Those displays

Have several regions which could gain focus (text access vicinity, checkboxes, listing of choices, ok and Cancel buttons), and the Tab key permits you to move from one to every other.

In graphical set up mode, you could use the mouse as you'll typically on an installed graphical desktop.

Figure 4.2

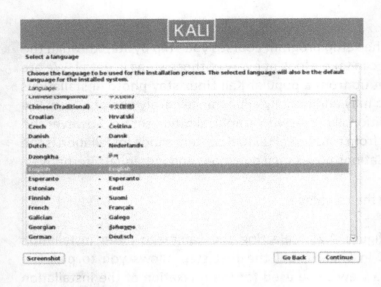

4.4.3 Selecting the Country

The second one step (Figure 4.3, "selecting the Country" is composed of choosing country. Blended with the language, this records enables the setup program to provide the most suitable keyboard format. This could additionally impact the configuration of the time sector. Inside the US, a Standard QWERTY keyboard is recommended, and the installer presents a choice of suitable time zones.

Figure 4.3

4.4.4 Selecting the Keyboard format

The proposed American English keyboard corresponds to the usual QWERTY layout as shown in Figure 4.4, "desire of Keyboard".

Figure 4.4

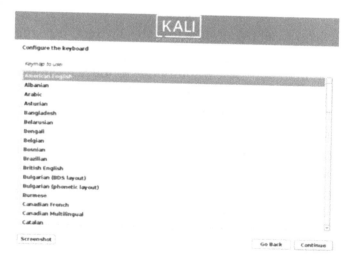

4.4.5 Detecting hardware

In the sizable majority of instances, the hardware detection step is completely computerized. The installer detects your hardware and tries to pick out the boot tool used which will get entry to its content. It loads the modules similar to the various hardware additives detected and then mounts the boot tool with the intention to examine it. The preceding steps have been absolutely contained inside the boot photo covered at the boot tool, a report of constrained length and loaded into memory with the aid of the bootloader when booting from the boot system.

4.4.6 Loading Components

With the contents of the boot system now to be had, the installer hundreds all the files essential to keep with its paintings. This consists of additional drivers for the final hardware (specifically the network card), in addition to all of the components of the installation application.

4.4.7 Detecting network hardware

In this step, the installer will try and automatically pick out the community card and cargo the corresponding module. If computerized detection fails, you can manually pick the module to load. If all else fails, you may load a particular module from a detachable system. This last solution is generally only wished if the best driving force isn't always covered within the standard Linux kernel, however, to be had somewhere else, including the manufacturer's website. This step should genuinely achieve success for community installations (inclusive of those finished when booting from a mini.iso), since the Debian applications must be loaded from the network.

4.4.8 Configuring the Network

As a way to automate the method as an awful lot as possible, the installer tries an automatic network configuration the use of Dynamic Host Configuration Protocol (DHCP) (for ipv4 and ipv6) and icmpv6's Neighbor Discovery Protocol (for ipv6), as proven in Figure , "network Autoconfiguration"

Figure 4.5

If the automatic configuration fails, the installer offers greater choices: attempt once more with a regular DHCP configuration, strive DHCP configuration by means of maintaining the call of the system, or installation a static community configuration.
This final choice requires an IP address, a subnet masks, an IP deal with for a capability gateway, a system name, and a site name.

4.4.9 user Creation

The installer prompts to create a new user (figure 4.6, "Create user") since it automatically creates a user account within the "sudo" organization. Which means the user has full administrative privileges via the sudo command. That is useful due to the reality that more than one objects are only to be had through administrative privileges. The installer also asks for a username for the account in addition to a password. The installer will request affirmation of the password to save you any input error.

Figure 4.6

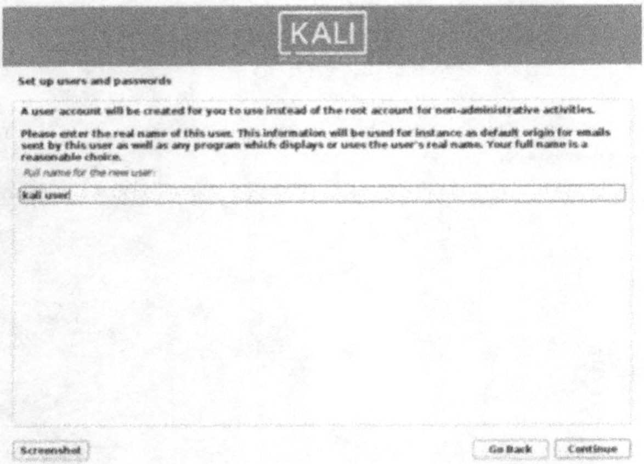

4.4.10 Configuring the Clock

If the community is available, the system's internal clock could be updated from a network time protocol (NTP) server. This is useful because it ensures timestamps on logs may be correct from the first boot.

In case your country spans more than one time zones, you may be asked to pick the time zone that you want to apply, as proven in figure 4.7, "Time zone choice"

Figure 4.7

4.5 Detecting Disks and Other Systems

This step mechanically detects the difficult drives on which Kali may be installed, each of so that you can be presented inside the subsequent step: partitioning.

Partitioning

Partitioning is a critical step in installation, which consists of dividing the available space on the difficult drives into discrete sections (walls) consistent with the intended feature of the desktop and those walls. Partitioning also entails choosing the report systems for use. All of those decisions may have a power on performance, information safety, and server management.

The partitioning step is historically tough for new users. However, the Linux report systems and partitions, including virtual memory (or swap partitions) need to be described as they shape the foundation of the gadget. This project can end up complicated when you have already hooked up another working system at the gadget and also you want the two to coexist. In this situation, you should make certain not to regulate its walls, or if want be, resize them without causing damage. To house greater common (and less complicated) partition schemes, maximum customers will choose the Guided mode that recommends partition configurations and provides suggestions each step of the manner. More advanced users will respect the manual mode, which lets in for greater superior configurations. Every mode shares certain abilities.

Guided Partitioning the primary display in the partitioning system (figure 4.8, "choice of Partitioning Mode") presents entry points for the guided and guide partitioning modes. "Guided use whole disk" is the most effective and most not unusual partition scheme, so that you can allocate an entire disk to Kali Linux.

The following two choices use Logical volume manager (LVM) to set up logical (instead of physical), optionally encrypted, walls.

Eventually, the remaining choice initiates guide partitioning, which allows for greater advanced partitioning schemes, inclusive of installing Kali Linux alongside other running systems. In this example, we will allocate a whole tough disk to Kali, so we choose "Guided use complete disk" to proceed to the next step.

Figure 4.8

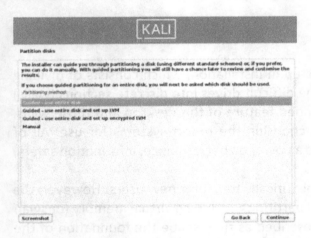

The subsequent display (proven in figure 4.9, "Disk to apply for Guided Partitioning" allows you to select the disk where Kali could be installed by means of deciding on the corresponding entry (for instance, "SCSI3 (0,0,0) (sda) 21.5 GB vmware, vmware virtual S"). Once decided on, guided partitioning will continue. This feature will erase all the statistics in this disk, so choose accurately.

Figure 4.9

Subsequent, the guided partitioning system gives 3 partitioning techniques, which correspond to different usages, as proven in parent 4.10, "Guided Partition Allocation"

Figure 4.10

The primary approach is known as "All files in one partition." The whole Linux system tree is saved in a single file system, similar to the root ("/") listing. This easy and strong partitioning scheme works flawlessly nicely for personal or single user structures. Despite the name, two walls will truly be created: the primary will house the complete gadget, the second the virtual reminiscence (or "swap"). The second one technique, "Separate /home/ temp partition," is comparable, however splits the record hierarchy in two: one partition contains the Linux system (/), and the second one incorporates "home directories" (meaning user facts, in files and subdirectories available under /home/). One benefit to this method is that it is simple to preserve the users' information when you have to reinstall the system. The remaining partitioning approach, known as "Separate /domestic, /var, and /temp partitions," is suitable for servers and multi user systems. It divides the record tree into many partitions: similarly, to the root (/) and user accounts (/home/) walls, it also has partitions for server software facts (/var/), and transient files (/temp/). One benefit to this method is that cease customers cannot lock up the server by using consuming all available difficult force area (they are able to only replenish /tmp/ and /domestic/). On the same time, service records (in particular logs) can now not clog up the rest of the system.

After choosing the form of partition, the installer presents a summary of your choices on the display screen as a partition map (figure 4.11, "Validating Partitioning") you could adjust every partition personally by means of selecting a partition. As an example, you can choose another record gadget if the usual (ext4) isn't suitable. In maximum cases, but the proposed partitioning is reasonable, and you may receive it by means of choosing "end partitioning and write modifications to disk." It may move without pronouncing, however pick out accurately as this will erase the contents of the chosen disk.

Figure 4.11

Chapter 5

5.1 Configuration of Kali Linux

5.2 Configuring the Network

In a standard desktop installation, you'll have Network Manager already set up and it is able to be controlled and configured through Xfce's system settings and via the top right menu as shown in figure 5.1, "Network Configuration system"

Figure 5.1

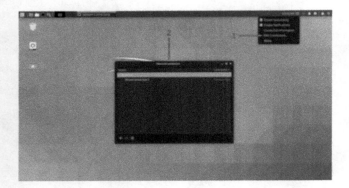

The default community configuration is predicated on DHCP to reap an IP deal with, DNS server, and gateway, but you can use the gear icon inside the lower left nook to regulate the configuration in many approaches (as an instance: set the MAC cope with, transfer to a static setup, enable or disable ipv6, and add additional routes). You could create profiles to save more than one wired network configurations and without problems transfer among them. For wireless networks, their settings are robotically tied to their public identifier (SSID). Network Manager also handles connections by means of mobile broadband (WIFI extensive region community WWAN) and by way of modems the use of on point protocol over ethernet (pppoe). Last but now not least, it offers integration with many sorts of virtual nonpublic networks (VPN) via committed plugins: SSH, open vpn, Cisco's VPNC, PPTP, Strong swan. Take a look at out the network manager* applications; most of them are not mounted by means of default.

5.2.1 On Command Line with Ifupdown

As an alternative, while you decide upon no longer to use (or don't have access to) a graphical desktop, you could configure the network with the already installed ifupdown package deal, which includes the ifup and ifdown tools. These tools examine definitions from the /and so forth/community/interfaces configuration report and are at the coronary heart of the /etc/init.d/networking init script that configures the network at boot time.

Every network device managed by using ifupdown may be de configured at any time with ifdown network device. You may then alter /and so forth/community/interfaces and produce the network again up (with the new configuration) with ifup network device.

Allow to take a look at what we are able to put in ifupdowns' configuration file. There are fundamental directives: automobile community device, which tells ifupdown to routinely configure the network interface once it is to be had, and iface network device inet/inet6 kind to configure a given interface.

auto lo   # DHCP configuration
Iface lo inet loopback   #the loopback network interface
auto eth0   #primary network interface
iface eth0 inet dhcp   #to get the ip

Notice that the special configuration for the loopback device need to constantly be found in this record. For a hard and fast IP address configuration, you need to provide greater information which includes the IP cope with, the network, and the IP of the gateway:

```
auto eth0              #primary network interface
Iface inet static
 address 192.168.1.18     #address
 netmask 255.255.255.0   #netmask
 broadcast 192.168.0.255  #broadcast
 network 192.168.0.0      #network
 gateway 192.168.1.1      #gateway
```

For WIFI interfaces, you should have the wpasupplicant package (included in Kali with the aid of default), which provides many wpa* alternatives that may be used in /etc/community/interfaces. Have a examine /usr/share/file/wpasupplicant/README.Debian.gz for examples and explanations. The most not unusual alternatives are wpa-ssid (which defines the name of the WIFI network to enroll in) and wpa psk (which defines the passphrase or the important thing protecting the community).

5.3 managing Unix users and Unix corporations

The database of Unix customers and companies includes the textual files /and so forth/passwd (list of customers), /etc/shadow (encrypted passwords of users), /and so forth/group (list of organizations), and /etc/gshadow (encrypted passwords of corporations). Their codecs are file in passwd(5), shadow(5), group(5), and gshadow(5) respectively while these files can be manually edited with gear like vipw and vigr, there are higher degree equipment to perform the most commonplace operations.

5.3.1 Creating User Accounts

Even though Kali is most often run at the same time as privileged with sudo permissions, you may regularly need to create unprivileged person bills for various reasons, specifically if you are using Kali as a primary operating machine. The most regular way to feature a user is with the adduser command, which takes a required argument: the username for the new user that you would like to create. The adduser command asks some questions earlier than creating the account but its usage is fairly honest. Its configuration record, /and so on/adduser.conf, includes many thrilling settings. You could, for example, define the variety of user identifiers (uids) that can be used, dictate whether or no longer users share a common institution or no longer, outline default shells, and greater.

The advent of an account triggers the population of the user's domestic directory with the contents of the /etc/skel/ template. This offers the user with a fixed of popular directories and configuration files. In a few cases, it'll be beneficial to add a user to a group (apart from their default foremost institution) so that it will furnish extra permissions. For example, a person who's included in the docker institution has complete access to docker commands and services. This will be completed with a command including adduser person group.

5.3.2 Modifying an existing Account or Password

The subsequent commands permit modification of the statistics saved in precise fields of the person databases:

- Passwd—permits a regular user to change their password, which in flip, updates the /and so forth/ shadow file.
- Chfn—(change full name), reserved for the quality super user(root), modifies the GECOS, or "general records" field.
- Chsh—(change shell) changes the consumer's login shell. But to be had selections will be limited to those indexed in /and so forth/shells; the administrator, alternatively, is not bound with the aid of this limit and can set the shell to any software chosen.
- Chage—(alternate AGE) lets in the administrator to exchange the password expiration settings via passing the username as an argument or listing present day settings the use of the -l person choice. As an alternative, you could also force the expiration of a password the use of the passwd -e user

command, which forces the person to trade their password the subsequent time they log in.

5.3.3 Disabling an Account

You may find yourself needing to disable an account (lock out a person) as a disciplinary measure, for the purposes of a research, or sincerely in the occasion of an extended or definitive absence of a consumer. A disabled account means the user can't login or gain access to the machine. The account remains intact at the system and no files or information are deleted; it's far definitely inaccessible. That is done by means of the use of the command passwd -l user(lock). Re enabling the account is completed in comparable style, with the -u choice (unlock release).

5.3.4 Management of Unix Groups

The add group and delgroup instructions add or delete a group, respectively. The groupmod command modifies a collection's information (its gid or identifier). The command gpasswdgroup modifications the password for the group, while the gpasswd -r organization command deletes it.

5.4 Configuration of Specific Program

On this segment we can take a look at offerings (now and again referred to as daemons), or applications that run as a heritage method and carry out diverse functions for the device. We can begin through discussing configuration documents and could continue to provide an explanation for how some important offerings (inclusive of SSH, postgresql, and Apache) feature and the way they can be configured. Kali Linux's policy is to have any community services disabled by default, which is a distinctive conduct to different Linux working systems.

5.4.1 Configuring a Specific Software Program

When you want to configure an unknown package deal, you should proceed in stages. The /usr/share/document/package/README. Debian document is a good location to start. This document will often include statistics approximately the package, which include hints that may refer you to different documentation. You will regularly store yourself quite a few time, and avoid numerous frustration, by means of reading this record first because it frequently details the maximum commonplace mistakes and solutions to most not unusual troubles. Next, you need to take a look at the software program's authentic documentation.. The dpkg -L package deal command gives a listing of files blanketed within the package deal; you may therefore quick pick out the to be had documentation (as well as the configuration documents, located in /etc/). Additionally, dpkg -s bundle presentations the package deal meta facts and indicates any viable advocated or suggested packages; in there, you may find documentation or possibly a utility with a purpose to ease the configuration of the software program. Finally, the configuration files are often self-documented by way of many explanatory feedback eliminating the various possible values for each configuration putting. In a few instances, you could get software up and running via uncommenting a single line within the configuration document. In other cases, examples of configuration documents are furnished inside the /usr/proportion/doc/package/examples/ directory. They'll function a basis on your own configuration file.

5.4.2 Configuring SSH Remote Logins

SSH permits you to remotely log into a system, transfer files, or execute commands. It is an industry standard device (ssh) and provider (sshd) for connecting to machines remotely.

While the openssh server package is hooked up by way of default, the SSH service is disabled by means of default and for that reason isn't always started out at boot time. You could manually begin the SSH provider with systemctl start ssh or configure it to begin at boot time with systemctl allow ssh. The SSH provider has a surprisingly sane default configuration, but given its effective abilities and sensitive nature, it is right to know what you can do with its configuration file, /and so forth/ssh/sshd_ config.

5.4.3 Configuring postgresql Databases

Postgresql is a database server. It is hardly ever beneficial on its very own but is used by many different offerings to shop statistics. Those services will generally get right of entry to the database server over the network and usually require authentication credentials which will join. Putting in those services therefore requires developing postgresql databases and person accounts with appropriate privileges at the database. Which will do this, we need the carrier to be going for walks, so permit's begin it with systemctl start postgresql.

5.5 Type of Connection and Client Authentication

By default, postgresql listens for incoming connections in two ways: on TCP port 5432 of the local host interface and on report primarily based socket /var/run/postgresql/.s.PGSQL.5432. This can be configured in postgresql.conf with various directives: listen_addresses for the addresses to pay attention to, port for the TCP port, and unix_socket_directories to outline the listing where the record-based sockets are created.

Depending on how they join, clients are authenticated in extraordinary ways. The pg_hba.conf configuration report defines who is allowed to connect on each socket and how they're authenticated. By default, connections on the file-based socket use the Unix user account because the name of the postgresql user, and it assumes that not similarly authentication is needed. On the TCP connection, postgresql calls for the consumer to authenticate with a username and a password (though now not a Unix username/password but as an alternative one controlled by postgresql itself).The postgres user is special and has complete administrative privileges over all databases. We can use this identity to create new customers and new databases.

5.6 creating Users and Databases

The create user command provides a new person and drop user gets rid of one. Likewise, the createdb command adds a new database and dropdb eliminates one. Every of those instructions have their personal manual pages but we are able to talk a number of the options here. Every command acts at the default cluster (strolling on port 5432) but you can pass --port=port to modify customers and databases of a alternate cluster. These instructions have to connect to the postgresql server to do their task and that they must be authenticated as a consumer with enough privileges which will execute the desired operation.

5.7 Managing Postgresql Clusters

First, it is well worth noting that the concept of "postgresql cluster" is a Debian specific addition and that you may not find any reference to this time period inside the legit postgresql documentation. From the factor of view of the postgresql tools, this sort of cluster is just an instance of a database server jogging on a specific port.

That said, Debian's postgresql common package deal affords a couple of tools to manage such clusters: pg_createcluster, pg_dropcluster, pg_ctlcluster, pg_upgradecluster, pg_renamecluster, and pg_lsclusters. We won't cowl all those gear here, but you can seek advice from their respective guide pages for more information. What you should understand is that when a new main model of postgresql gets installed to your system, it's going to create a new cluster in an effort to run on the next port (commonly 5433) and you may hold the usage of the old model until you migrate your databases from the old cluster to the brand new one.

5.8 Configuring Apache

An ordinary Kali Linux installation consists of the Apache net server, supplied by the apache package. Being a community service, it is disabled through default. You may manually begin it with systemctl start apache. With increasingly applications being disbursed as internet programs, it is vital to have some understanding of Apache in order to host the ones programs, whether for local utilization or for making them to be had over the network.

Apache is a modular server, and many functions are applied by outside modules that the principal application hundreds during its initialization. The default configuration handiest permits the maximum not unusual modules, however enabling new modules is without difficulty finished by running a2enmod module. Use a2dismod module to disable a module. These programs definitely most effective create (or delete) symbolic links in /and so on/apache2/mods enabled/, pointing at the real files (saved in /and so forth/apache2/ mods to be had/). There are numerous modules available, however two are really worth initial consideration: php and SSL (used for TLS). Web programs written with php are completed by way of the Apache internet server with the assist of the committed module furnished by means of the libapache mod Hypertext Preprocessor bundle, and its set up routinely allows the module.

5.9 Service Management

Kali uses systemd as its init system, which is not only accountable for the boot series, but also permanently acts as a complete featured service manager, starting and monitoring services. Systemd can be queried and managed with systemctl. With no argument, it runs the systemctl list units command, which outputs a list of the active units. If you run systemctl fame, the output indicates a hierarchical assessment of the jogging offerings. Evaluating both out places, you straight away see that there are multiple forms of gadgets and that services are most effective considered one of them. Each service is represented by means of a service unit, that is defined by using a carrier document commonly shipped in /lib/systemd/device/ (or /run/systemd/gadget/, or /and many others/systemd/machine/; they're listed via increasing order of importance, and the final one wins). Each is likely modified by different carrier name.service.d/*.conf documents inside the same set of directories. The ones unit files are undeniable text documents whose layout is inspired by means of the known "*.ini" files of Microsoft windows, with key = fee pairs grouped between [segment] headers.

Chapter 6

6.1 Kali Linux: Securing and Monitoring

6.2 Security Policy

It is impractical to discuss security in vast strokes since the concept represents a huge range of concepts, tools, and tactics, none of which practice universally. Selecting amongst them requires a unique idea of what your desires are. Securing a gadget starts off evolved with answering some questions. Running headlong into imposing an arbitrary set of tools runs the hazard of focusing on the wrong components of protection. Additionally, it is best to determine a selected goal. A great method to assist with that dedication starts with the subsequent questions:

- What is the thing you want to protect? Security policy differs in sense what you want to secure computers or data. Inside the latter case, you furthermore might need to realize which records.
- What are you looking to defend against? Is it leakage of exclusive data and facts? Accidental loss of data? Loss of revenue because of disruption of service?
- Additionally, who are you looking to protect towards? Security features will be pretty distinct for guarding towards a typo through an everyday person of the gadget as opposed to defensive in opposition to a determined external attacker institution.

The time period "danger" is customarily used to refer together to these 3 factors: what to defend, what need to be avoided, and who may make this show up. Modeling the risk calls for solutions to those 3 questions. From this chance model, a safety coverage may be built, and the coverage can be implemented with concrete movements. More constraints are also well worth thinking of as they could restrict the range of available rules. How some distance are you willing to go to at ease a machine? This query has a primary impact on which coverage to put into effect. Too often, the solution is most effective described in terms of economic expenses, however other elements must also be considered, consisting of the quantity of inconvenience imposed on tools users or overall performance degradation.

As soon as the threat has been modeled, you may begin thinking about designing a real protection policy. There are extremes that may come into play when identifying the level of safety protections to undertake. On one hand, it can be extremely simple to provide basic system safety. As an instance, if the gadget to be covered handiest comprises a secondhand computer, the only use of which is to add some numbers on the end of the day, figuring out now not to do something special to defend it'd be quite affordable. The intrinsic value of the machine is low, and the value of the facts are zero given that they're not saved on the computer. A potential attacker infiltrating this device might only benefit a calculator. The price of securing one of these gadget might probably be more than the fee of a breach.

At the opposite give up of the spectrum, you might need to guard the confidentiality of mystery facts within the most complete manner possible, trumping another consideration. In this example, an appropriate response would be the overall destruction of the facts (securely erasing the files, shredding of the difficult disks to bits, then dissolving those bits in acid, and so forth). If there is a further requirement that facts should be kept in keep for future use (despite the fact that not necessarily comfortably available), and if value nonetheless isn't a factor, then a place to begin could be storing the information on iridium platinum alloy plates stored in bomb proof bunkers under numerous mountains inside the world, each of which being (of path) both entirely secret and protected by means of complete armies.

Extreme though these examples may additionally appear, they would nevertheless be a good enough response to certain described risks, insofar as they are the outcome of a concept manner that takes into consideration the dreams to reach and the limitations to satisfy. When coming from a reasoned selection, no safety coverage is greater, or less, first rate than some other.

Coming back to a more traditional case, a records device may be segmented into constant and typically independent subsystems. Every subsystem could have its personal requirements and constraints, and so the risk assessment and the layout of the safety policy ought to be undertaken one at a time for each. An excellent precept to preserve in mind is that a small attack surface is simpler to guard than a big one. The community organization must additionally be designed therefore: the touchy offerings should be targeting a small quantity of machines, and those machines have to only be accessible via a minimal quantity of routes or test factors. The common sense is straightforward: it's miles less difficult to comfortable those checkpoints than to relaxed all the touchy machines against everything of the outdoor international. It's miles at this factor that the usefulness of community filtering (which include by means of firewalls) becomes apparent. This filtering may be carried out with committed hardware, but an easier and greater flexible answer is to apply a software firewall such as the one integrated within the Linux kernel.

6.3 Possible Security Measures

As the preceding phase explained, there may be no unmarried reaction to the query of the way to comfortable Kali Linux. It all relies upon on how you operate it and what you are attempting to protect.

6.3.1 On a Server

If you run Kali Linux on a publicly accessible server, you maximum in all likelihood want to at secure network services by converting any default passwords that is probably configured. If you hand out user debts either without delay on the server or on one of the offerings, you need to make certain that you set sturdy passwords (they should withstand brute force assaults). At the identical time, you would possibly want to setup fail2ban, a good way to make it a lot harder to brute force passwords over the community (via filtering away IP addresses that exceed a restriction of failed login attempts). Installation fail2ban with apt replace followed through apt deploy fail2ban. In case you run web services, you probably need to host them over HTTPS to save you community intermediaries from sniffing your traffic (which would possibly encompass authentication cookies).

6.3.2 On a laptop

The computer of a penetration tester is not subject to the identical risks as a public server: as an instance, you are much less probable to be situation to random scans from script kiddies or even whilst you are, you possibly won't have any community offerings enabled.

Real threat often arises while you journey from one customer to the next. For instance, your computer will be stolen even as travelling or seized via customs. This is why you maximum possibly need to use full disk encryption and probable also setup the "nuke" the records that you have accrued for the duration of your engagements are confidential and require the maximum safety.

You could also want firewall policies but no longer for the same purpose as on the server. You might need to forbid all outbound traffic except the traffic generated by means of your VPN access. This is supposed as a safety internet, so that after the VPN is down, you immediately notice it (instead of falling lower back to the nearby community get right of entry to). That manner, you do not disclose the IP addresses of your clients while you browse the internet or do different online activities. Similarly, in case you are performing a nearby inner engagement, it's far nice to remain on top of things of all of your pastime to lessen the noise you create at the community, that may alert the customer and their defense structures.

6.4 Securing Network Offerings

In general, it is a great idea to disable offerings that you do no longer use. Kali makes it easy to do this on the grounds that network offerings are disabled via default.

As long as services stay disabled, they do no longer pose any protection danger. But you need to be careful whilst you allow them because:

- There is no firewall by default, so if they listen on all network interfaces, they are effectively publicly to be had.
- A few offerings don't have any authentication credentials and assist you to set them on first use; others have default (and hence well known) credentials preset. Ensure to (re)set any password to something that best you know.
- Many services run as root with full administrator privileges, so the effects of unauthorized get entry to or a safety breach are consequently generally severe.

6.5 Firewall or Packet Filtering

A firewall is a chunk of computer system with hardware, software program, or each that parses the incoming or outgoing network packets (coming to or leaving from a nearby community) and most effective lets via the ones matching certain predefined situations.

A filtering community gateway is a form of firewall that protects an entire community. Additionally, it is established on a committed device configured as a gateway for the network so that it may parse all packets that skip inside and out of the network. As a substitute, a local firewall is a software provider that runs on one precise gadget so that it will clear out or restriction get admission to some services on that machine, or possibly to prevent outgoing connections with the aid of rogue software program that a person should, willingly or not, have mounted.

The Linux kernel embeds the netfilter firewall. There's no turnkey solution for configuring any firewall due to the fact that network and user requirements vary. But you can manipulate netfilter from user area with the iptables and ip6tables commands. The distinction among these two instructions is that the previous works for ipv4 networks, whereas the latter works on ipv6. Due to the fact that both network protocol stacks will in all likelihood be around for decades, both gear will want to be used in parallel. You could also use the splendid GUI based fwbuilder tool, which offers a graphical representation of the filtering regulations. But you make a decision to configure it, netfilter is Linux's firewall implementation, so let's take a closer observe how it works.

6.5.1 Netfilter behavior

Netfilter makes use of four distinct tables, which shop rules regulating 3 types of operations on packets:

- Filter out concerns filtering policies (accepting, refusing, or ignoring a packet).
- Nat (Network address Translation) issues translation of supply or destination addresses and ports of packets.
- Mangle issues other modifications to the IP packets (including the tos form of service field and options).
- Raw permits different manual modifications on packets earlier than they reach the relationship tracking system.

Each table includes lists of guidelines known as chains. The firewall uses standard chains to deal with packets based on predefined circumstances. The administrator can create other chains, if you want to simplest be used while referred through certainly one of the standard chains (either without delay or circuitously).
The filter table has three known chains:

- INPUT: issues packets whose vacation spot is the firewall itself.
- OUTPUT: concerns packets emitted through the firewall.
- Ahead: concerns packets passing through the firewall (which is neither their source nor their destination).

The Nat desk also has three popular chains:
- PREROUTING: to modify packets as quickly as they come.
- POSTROUTING: to modify packets whilst they are ready to go on their way.
- OUTPUT: to alter packets generated by using the firewall itself.

These chains are illustrated in figure 6.1, "How Netfilter Chains are referred to as"

Figure 6.1

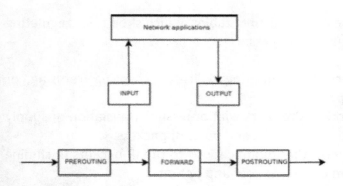

Every chain is a listing of regulations; every rule is a hard and fast of situations and an action to perform when the situations are met. Whilst processing a packet, the firewall scans the right chain, one rule after some other, and when the conditions for one rule are met, it jumps to the desired movement to preserve processing. The most commonplace behaviors are standardized, and dedicated moves exist for them. Taking this sort of standard actions interrupts the processing of the chain, since the packets fate is already sealed (barring an exception mentioned under). Indexed below are the Netfilter movements.

- **ACCEPT**: allow the packet to move on its way.
- **REJECT:** reject the packet with a web manipulate message protocol (ICMP) error packet
- (the --reject-with kind choice of iptables determines the kind of error to ship).
- **DROP:** delete (ignore) the packet.
- **LOG:** log (via syslog) a message with an outline of the packet. Be aware that this action does now not interrupt processing, and the execution of the chain maintains at the following rule, which is why

logging refused packets requires each a LOG and a REJECT/DROP rule. Common parameters related to logging include:

- --log-level, with default value warning, indicates the syslog severity level.
- --log-prefix allows specifying a textual content prefix to distinguish among logged messages.
- --log-tcp-sequence, --log-tcp-options, and --log-ip-options indicate extra records to be integrated into the message: respectively, the TCP sequence quantity, TCP options, and IP alternatives.

- **ULOG:** log a message through ulogd, which may be higher adapted and greater efficient than syslogd for managing huge numbers of messages; be aware that this movement, like LOG, also returns processing to the following rule inside the calling chain.
- **Chain_name:** jump to the given chain and compare its policies.
- **RETURN:** interrupt processing of the cutting-edge chain and return to the calling chain; in case the modern chain is a preferred one, there's no calling chain, so the default motion (defined with the -P choice to iptables) is achieved alternatively.
- **SNAT** (only within the Nat table): practice supply community address Translation (SNAT). Extra options describe the exact adjustments to apply, such as to the source cope with port option, which defines the new supply IP address and/or port.
- **DNAT** (most effective within the nat table): practice vacation spot community deal with Translation (DNAT). Greater options describe the exact adjustments to use, which includes to the destination cope with port choice, which defines the new destination IP cope with and/or port.
- **MASQUERADE** (only in the nat table): apply masquerading (a special case of supply NAT).
- **REDIRECT** (simplest in the nat table): transparently redirect a packet to a given port of the firewall itself; this will be used to set up a transparent web proxy that works and not using a configuration on the client side, for the reason that consumer thinks it connects to the recipient while the communications

absolutely undergo the proxy. To the ports port(s) choice suggests the port, or port range, where the packets need to be redirected.

6.5.2 Syntax of iptables and ip6tables

The iptables and ip6tables commands are used to control tables, chains, and guidelines.
Their -t table option suggests which table to perform on (by way of default, filter out).

Commands

The main alternatives for interacting with chains are indexed underneath:

- -L chain lists the policies inside the chain. That is commonly used with the -n choice to disable name resolution (for instance, iptables -n -L input will show the rules related to in- coming packets).
- -N chain creates a new chain. New chains can be made for multiple purposes, such as checking out a new network carrier or averting a community attack.
- -X chain deletes an empty and unused chain (as an example, iptables -X ddos-attack).
- -A chain rule provides a rule at the give up of the given chain. Take into account that guidelines are processed from top to bottom so be sure to keep this in thoughts when including regulations.
- -I chain rule_num inserts a rule right before the rule number rule_num. As with the -A option, maintain the processing order in thoughts whilst placing new guidelines into a series.
- -D chain rule_num(or -D chain rule) it deletes the rule present in a chain: the very first syntax identifies the rule to be deleted by its wide variety (iptables -L –line numbers will show those numbers), at the same time as the latter identifies it by using its contents.
- -F chain flushes a sequence (deletes all its policies). As an instance, to delete all the guidelines associated with outgoing packets, you'll run iptables -F OUTPUT. If no chain is stated, all of the policies in the table are deleted.

- -P chain defines the action which is default action, or some "policy" for any given chain it is important to note that only standard chains may have such a coverage. To drop all incoming site visitors via default, you would run iptables -P enter DROP.

Rules

Every rule is expressed as situations -j action action_options. If several situations are described in the identical rule, then the criterion is the conjunction (logical AND) of the conditions, that is at least as restrictive as every person circumstance.

The -p protocol condition suits the protocol subject of the IP packet. The maximum not unusual values are tcp, udp, icmp, and icmpv6. This condition can be complemented with situations at the TCP ports, with clauses consisting of –support -port port and –destination-port port.

6.5.3 Creating Rules

Each rule introduction calls for one invocation of iptables or ip6tables. Typing these commands manually can be tedious, so the calls are commonly stored in a script in order that the device is automatically configured the same manner whenever the device boots. This script may be written through hand however it is able to additionally be thrilling to put together it with an excessive degree tool together with fwbuilder. The principle is straightforward. In the first step, describe all of the factors on the way to be concerned within the actual regulations:

- Servers
- with its network interfaces, the firewall itself
- with the corresponding IP ranges, the network
- belonging ports to the services only hosted on the servers

Then the action wishes to be selected and configured.As far as ipv6 is concerned, you could both create distinct rulesets for ipv4 and ipv6, or create most effective one and allow fwbuilder translate the regulations in step with the addresses assigned to the items. Fwbuilder will generate a script configuring the firewall according to the policies which you have defined. Its modular structure offers it the capability to generate scripts targeting distinctive structures along with iptables for Linux, ipf for freebsd, and pf for OpenBSD.

Figure 6.2

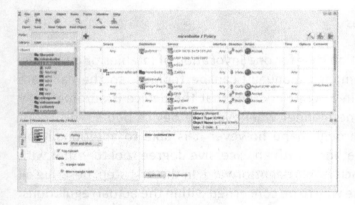

6.5.4 Installing in the rules at every Boot

So that you can put into effect the firewall rules on every occasion the machine is booted, you will want to sign in the configuration script in an up directive of the /and so forth/community/interfaces document. Within the following example, the script is stored under /usr/nearby/etc/awais.fw (awais being the hostname of the machine).

Auto eth0 #primary network interface

Iface inet static
Address 192.168.1.18   #address
Netmask 255.255.255.0   #netmask
Broadcast 192.168.0.255 #broadcast
Network 192.168.0.0   #network
Gateway 192.168.1.1   #gateway
Up/usr/nearby/etc/awais.fw

This case assumes which you are using ifupdown to configure the network interfaces. In case you are the use of something else (like network manager or systemd-networkd), then refer to their respective documentation to discover ways to execute a script after the interface has been added up.

6.6 Logging and Monitoring

Data confidentiality and protection is a crucial thing of safety, but it is similarly critical to ensure availability of offerings. As an administrator and safety practitioner, you have to ensure that the whole lot works as expected, and it is your obligation to locate anomalous behavior and provider degradation in a timely way. Tracking and logging software plays a key function on this component of security, imparting perception into what's happening on the system and the network. In this segment, we can evaluation a few equipment that may be used to reveal several components of a Kali gadget.

6.6.1 monitoring Logs with logcheck

The logcheck application monitors log files each hour by way of default and sends unusual log messages in emails to the administrator for further analysis. The listing of monitored documents is stored in /etc/logcheck/logcheck.logfiles. The default values
Paintings excellent if the /and so forth/rsyslog.conf file has no longer been absolutely overhauled. Logcheck can report in numerous degrees of element: paranoid, server, and notebook. Paranoid is very verbose and should likely be constrained to unique servers which include firewalls. Server is the default mode and is recommended for

maximum servers. Notebook is obviously designed for workstations and is extremely terse, filtering out greater messages than the opposite options. In all three cases, logcheck must probably be customized to exclude some greater messages (depending on set up offerings), except you actually need to receive hourly batches of lengthy uninteresting emails. Because the message choice mechanism is as an alternative complex, /usr/share/document/ logcheck database/README.logcheck database.gz is a required if difficult study.

6.6.2 Monitoring Interest in Real Time

Top is an interactive device that shows a listing of currently running approaches. The default sorting is based on the contemporary amount of processor use and can be acquired with the P key. Different sort orders consist of a sort by occupied reminiscence (M key), by way of general processor time (T key), and by way of method identifier (N key). The k key kills a process via coming into its method identifier. The r key modifications the priority of a manner. When the gadget appears to be overloaded, top is an incredible tool to see which approaches are competing for processor time or consuming an excessive amount of memory. Mainly, it's miles frequently thrilling to check if the methods ingesting resources healthy the actual offerings that the machine is thought to host. An unknown system walking because the "www - records" consumer ought to virtually stand out and be investigated since it's likely an example of software established and completed at the system thru a vulnerability in a web utility. Top is a completely flexible device, and its manual web page offers information on the way to customize its display and adapt it to your private desires and habits. The xfce4v task manager graphical tool is just like pinnacle and it affords roughly the equal features. For GNOME users there is gnome system screen and for KDE users there is ksysguard which can be each comparable as nicely.

Chapter 7

7.1 Advanced Usage

7.2 Modifying Kali Packages

Enhancing Kali applications is mostly an assignment for Kali individuals and developers: they update packages with new upstream versions, they tweak the default configuration for a better integration in the distribution, or they fix insects suggested by customers. However, you may have precise needs not fulfilled by way of the official applications and understanding the way to construct a changed package can hence be very valuable.

You would possibly marvel why you want to bother with the package in any respect. In spite of everything, if you have to modify a piece of software program, you may usually seize its supply code (commonly with git) and run the changed version immediately from the supply checkout. This is excellent when it is feasible and while you use your private home listing for this cause, but if your software calls for a system wide setup (as an instance, with a make installation step) then it'll pollute your file gadget with documents unknown to dpkg and will quickly create problems that can't be stuck by way of bundle dependencies. Moreover, with proper packages you may be capable of proportion your changes and deploy them on multiple computers lots greater effortlessly or revert the adjustments after having discovered that they had been no longer operating in addition to you was hoping. So, when might you need to alter a package deal? Allows check a few examples. First, we will count on which you are a heavy person of Social Engineer Toolkit (SET) and you noticed a new upstream release however the Kali developers are all busy for a conference and you want to try it out right now. You want to update the bundle yourself. In every other case, we are able to expect which you are suffering to get your

MIFARE NFC card operating and also you need to rebuild "libfreefare" to allow debug messages to be able to have actionable information to provide in a worm file which you are presently preparing. In an ultimate case, we are able to assume that the "pyrit" software fails with a cryptic errors message. After a web search, you find a commit which you count on to repair your trouble within the upstream github repository and also you want to rebuild the package with this repair applied. We can go through all of these samples within the following sections. We can try to generalize the reasons so you can higher follow the commands to other instances however it is impossible to cowl all situations which you might encounter. Something change you want to make; the overall system is continually the identical: take hold of the source percentage, extract it, make your changes, then build the bundle. However, for every step, there are often a couple of tools that could manage the challenge. We picked the most relevant and most famous tools, however our assessment isn't always exhaustive.

7.3 Getting the sources

Rebuilding a Kali package deal starts with getting its supply code. A supply package consists of a couple of files: the primary report is the *.dsc (Debian supply control) report as it lists the alternative accompanying documents, which may be *.tar.gz,bz2,xz, sometimes *.diff.gz, or *.debian.tar.gz,bz2,xz documents.
The supply packages are saved on Kali mirrors which are to be had over HTTP. You can use your web browser to download all of the required files but the easiest way to perform that is to use the apt supply source_package_name command. This command requires a deb -src line within the /etc/apt/sources.listing record and up to date index files (completed via strolling apt update).

7.3.1 Installing Build Dependencies

Now which you have the assets, you continue to want to install construct dependencies. They'll be essential to construct the favored binary packages but also are possibly required for partial builds which you may want to run to test the adjustments at the same time as you're making them.

7.3.2 Making changes

We can't cover all of the possible changes that you might need to make to a given package in this phase. This would quantity to coaching you all of the nitty gritty info of Debian packaging. However, we are able to cover the 3 common use cases provided earlier and we will give an explanation for some of the unavoidable parts (like maintaining the changelog file). The first thing to do is to change the package version variety so that the rebuilt applications can be prominent from the authentic programs provided by way of Debian or Kali. To reap this, we typically add a suffix figuring out the entity (person or organization) making use of the changes. This invokes a text editor (sensible editor, who runs the editor assigned within the visual or EDITOR environment variables, or /usr/bin/editor otherwise), which permits you to document the differences added via this rebuild.

7.3.3 Applying a Patch

In considered one of our use instances, we've downloaded the pyrit supply package and we want to apply a patch that we found in the upstream Git repository. This is a commonplace operation and it have too always been simple. Lamentably, patches may be handled in special methods relying on the supply bundle format and at the Git packaging workflow in use (when Git is used to maintain the package).

7.3.4 Tweaking Build Options

You normally have to tweak construct alternatives when you want to enable an elective feature or behavior that is not activated within the reputable bundle, or while you need to personalize parameters that are set at construct time via a ./configure alternative or via variables set in the build environment. In those cases, the modifications are typically restrained to debian/regulations, which drives the steps within the package build process. Inside the simplest cases, the lines concerning the preliminary configuration (./configure) or the actual build ($(MAKE) or make) are easy to identify. If these commands are not explicitly called, they're in all likelihood a facet impact of every other specific command, in which case, please confer with their documentation to examine greater approximately how to change the default behavior. With packages while the usage of dh, you would possibly need to feature an override for the dh_auto_configure or dh_auto_build commands.

7.4 Recompiling the Linux Kernel

The kernels furnished by means of Kali encompass the largest viable range of features, as well as the maximum variety of drivers, to be able to cover the broadest spectrum of current hardware configurations. That is why some users choose to recompile the kernel which will consist of simplest what they in particular need. There are reasons for this preference. First, it's miles a manner to optimize reminiscence intake on the grounds that all kernel code, even though it's far never used, occupies bodily memory. Due to the fact the statically compiled quantities of the kernel are never moved to swap area, a typical lower in system overall performance will result from having drivers and functions built in that are by no means used. Second, decreasing the wide variety of drivers and kernel features reduces the threat of security troubles considering the fact that simplest a fraction of the available kernel code is being run.

7.4.1 Introduction and prerequisites

Unsurprisingly, Debian and Kali manage the kernel within the shape of a package deal, which isn't how kernels have historically been compiled and hooked up. For the reason that kernel stays underneath the manipulate of the packaging gadget, it could then be removed cleanly, or deployed on several machines. Furthermore, the scripts associated with these programs automate the interaction with the bootloader and the initrd generator.

7.4.2 Getting the resources

Because the Linux kernel resources are available as a bundle, you can retrieve them by way of putting in the Linux sources model package. The apt -cache seek ^Linux -source command need to list the modern kernel model packaged by Kali. Be aware that the supply code contained in these applications does now not correspond exactly with that published by Linus Torvalds and the kernel developers; like all distributions, Debian and Kali observe some of patches, which may (or might not) locate their manner into the upstream model of Linux. These changes encompass backports of fixes/features/drivers from newer kernel variations, new functions not but (completely) merged in the upstream Linux tree, and now and again even Debian or Kali specific adjustments.

7.5 Compiling and constructing the Package

Once the kernel configuration is ready, a simple make deb -pkg will generate as much as 5 Debian programs in fashionable .deb layout: Linux image version, which incorporates the kernel photo and the associated modules; Linux headers model, which includes the header documents required to build external modules; linux firmware image model, which includes the firmware files needed through a few drivers (this package deal is probably missing whilst you construct from the kernel assets supplied through Debian or Kali); linux image modeld bg, which contains the debugging symbols for the kernel photo and its modules; and linux libc dev, which includes headers applicable to some user space libraries like GNU's C library (glibc).

Conclusion

Congratulations you have done tremendous and have learnt much about Kali Linux system. And you should use it in various projects to get hold of the knowledge. You have discovered and learnt interesting features of Kali Linux and know that they have some limitations, and you need to work around those limitations. With constantly changing distributions and boost of technology everyday some part of the book become older, so you need to keep up with the knowledge.

CPSIA information can be obtained
at www.ICGtesting.com
Printed in the USA
LVHW051413250621
691051LV00005B/417